T0161109

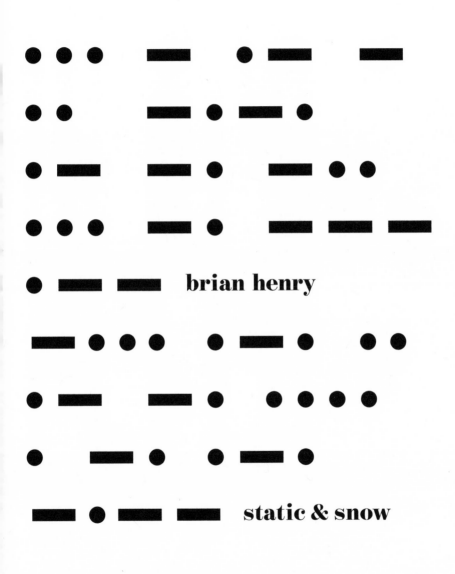

brian henry

static & snow

Static & Snow

Brian Henry

Black Ocean
Boston · Detroit · Chicago

Black Ocean
P.O. Box 52030
Boston, MA 02205
blackocean.org

Cover Art and Design by Abby Haddican | abbyhaddican.com
Book Design by Nikkita Cohoon | nikkita.co

ISBN 978-1-939568-12-0

Library of Congress Cataloging-in-Publication Data

Henry, Brian, 1972-
 [Poems. Selections]
 Static & snow / Brian Henry.
    pages ; cm
 ISBN 978-1-939568-12-0 (acid-free paper)
 I. Title. II. Title: Static and snow.
 PS3608.E566A6 2015
 811'.6-dc23
                                        2015029859

FIRST EDITION

CONTENTS

ACKNOWLEDGMENTS

Some of these poems have appeared in the following magazines: *Conjunctions* (web), *Connotation*, *Denver Quarterly*, *Front Porch*, *Guernica*, *Handsome*, *Interim*, *The Laurel Review*, *The Modern Review* (Canada), *New American Writing*, *Poetry Daily*, *A Public Space*, *Shearsman* (UK), *Transom*, *Tyger Burning*, *Volt*, *The Wolf* (UK), and *Zoland Poetry*.

Many thanks to their editors.

Thanks, too, to *Poetry Daily* for reprinting "River Crossing" and to *Verse Daily* for selecting "Elegy Elegy" as a weekly feature.

"What Vista" was produced as a broadside by Smokey Road Press in collaboration with the University of North Georgia.

"Moth Ark" received the 2008 Cecil B. Hemley Memorial Award, judged by Norma Cole.

"Day is wreathed in what summer lost."
—Basil Bunting, *Briggflatts*

In memoriam
Tomaž Šalamun (1941–2014)

The river's candle
clipped by the footbridge
that pins the rockedge,
an island of water
patient to rejoin
what surrounds it.
Your breath—air held,
extended between—
draws and drowns us
under a runt sun.
We trumple the muck,
through the lumpen
summer muck, tracked
by an angry grackle's
grace note: it strangles
our stride, our stricken,
sickly stride, static
in that string of song.

FIRST SNOW

Who among us

is alive

a temporary ailment

between nil and naught

instance of matter

illusion of same

detour this condition

what route to take

no sight to lean on

some arc uncontained

what are we

who loiter through

*

What falls

when it melts

the ground so minor

the smallest shadow

could cover

one hand to hold

one hand to shape

the wet into place

beneath the rays

that drag the eye

along every shard

and absent trace

*

Astride the level field

of borrowed light

instance of sorrow

spent with the sun

open upon a blaze

to deter a frantic moon

you tilt your mouth

unward and decline

how you move

across the snow

across without sinking

horizon-drawn surface

WHAT VISTA

—and the clouds moved on

               with their rain

after six days of static

                     o-

pening the wind

              -stroked river on

the underside of the bridge

                   arc-

ing over. The river

                flickered

on the stone, grime-

        stricken but, from here,

smooth, the river

             flickered, and

nothing, you thought,

       could move there, where

no bank or boat

         could work, provide

a point whence to view.

                If only

the bridge &/or those

              crossing it

could see what belongs,

             at least now

(and only) to you.

                If only.

BLANK POSTCARD

I've forgotten how to connect,
the basics
        on which everything meaningful
is built.
        A month passes, another, a year,
and still
        I simmer in my own pot
of failure.
        This vow of obliscence, who
imposed it?
        Who banned the minor chords as well
as speech?
        The simplest gesture, slightest touch
or glance?
        Inside me everything, I'm told,
is fine.
        Nothing abnormal about my waves,
my eyes.
        The shoreline squints from below,
is pinched.

Even the clouds find it brainless
to gather

and, by gathering, to engage.
Or connect.

Is it prohibited to call oneself
an isthmus?

A strip of something solid, dangling,
mid air?

RIVER RIVER

What burden
the mountains

some curtain
gone wrong

cracked horizon
some vista

collapsible incline
now undone

a body
without use

some thickness
or failure

what vista
river gesture

RIVER BOTTOM

Like a face you know
it's there
without seeing it

but without that shock
when a mirror
confirms it.

RIVER SONG

I stand in the water

the water this river

I stand in the water

the water this river

I stand in the water

the water this river

and the sky it goes silver

I stand in the water

the water this silver

I stand in the water

the water this water

I stand in the river

the river no water

I stand in the river

NO FISHING

where leaffall and twigs
cluster until

a heavy rain's weighty
inertia

unclogs to rut a detour
via compost and clover—

*

The honey ant's fluid motions
go fuzzy

                    cigarette butt
                    cellophane
                    cigarette butt

Some kind of pod split
open
                              emptied

*

The turtles drop
            in succession
from their spots
                      treefall and log
youngest to oldest
when the human stops
            to watch and hear
here at this break
                      in shorebrush
where what's audible
becomes visible
                      vista

RIVER CROSSING

There, where stones populate
the underneath, splay
rain as it blends and stops
being rain, raises the river,
water into water, stone
into soil, too slick to stand
or walk, too wide to freeze
or span, to cross you must
swim, the current a visible
instance of movement:
you'd enter the water here
and if not pulled under
would emerge so far downstream
the crossing would require
another journey entirely,
on foot, over uncertain terrain,
over what, through ownership,
through deed, is called property,
thus encroachment, thus trespass.

The mind, though, can cross,

along with the eye (where it can see).

The body, my dear, counts

for so little—nothing, really—here.

RIVER BORDER

On one side of the bridge, rapids.
On the other side, water
seeming still. You there
in the middle, neither
moving nor still. The river
has no borders, it is
the border. The bank
has no hold on the water.
The bank is dirt, and rock,
and is worked by water.
You can walk along the river
but not in it. The water
would bear you with it,
rescind your feet's hold
on the bottom. The river
bears whatever's there.
The river does not move,
it goes. It goes nowhere,
from nowhere to nowhere.

OCTOBERY FEBRUARY

Distrust what the eyes bring,
nothing that soft can stand
up to the sight of what ends
only to begin again.
Tiepolo knew the difference
between sky and *sky*. (Broken
sight). Schuyler, too. The garden's
sharpest scholar. Here, even
the shadows are tarnished.
Sad gray rows that seem to know
they serve no purpose.
They have no smell, make
no sound, feel like nothing
but what they're cast upon,
taste like nothing but what
they're cast upon. So much
weaker than wind, snow, glare
on the snow, they live
on borrowed surfaces.
There's no bottom to them
when sky and ground
share the same hue.

BRIGHT INVITING

The river pulps the tree that fell, already dead,
onto a rock, holding the tree there, horizontal
in the river air, unmoving in the river's glare.

The snow melts upon contact with the water,
the snow melts upon contact with the rock but clings
to the tree and the ice briefly before it melts.

The river takes it all in. A pillar of salt knocked over:
how long will it stay on its side? At least until spring,
when the river will rise, quicken, and take any thing with it.

The unreached shore reflects the river's thinking.
Sound/unsound the rapids, hinge/unhinge the rock,
only ice can polish what rears above water,

only ice can skirt the rock.
                                    The tree points
as if to push the river wider, an accusing finger
hurled at the bank: *the small earth cannot just file past*

*the bracing flood-breath of another planet as if nothing
has happened.*
                                    A birdless tree, a sky without birds.
A forked tongue above the river, it flickers

toward the shore but licks only air. In spring,
the water will quench it. Rot and shift it.
You do well, tree, to fade away as if at a border crossing,

fashioning your vanishing to end without force
in a minimum, rocking note.
                              Downstream, the bridge
frames all of this. Upstream, it effaces: the river

the bridge's afterthought, the tree the river's compass.
The river, you realize, fears contact:
                              to be touched
(angle, light, snow /
                    river, rock, tree)
                              is to be altered.

WINTER VIEW

Sometimes I face the sky.
Sometime I face
first in the snow.
No horse to guide
or pull me out
of, no horse to ride.
Dawn comes to he
who's stuck in place.
Dawn comes.

*

I move when I think
and now I cannot move.
My mind can grasp
anything when I move.
A map would be mine
within moments.
Any list or fact,
any scrap.
I could sing pi
to sixty places.
Here for months, here
my mind has only snow.
Fed nothing but snow.

*

If I could move
I would, of course,
I would move
without stopping
and my mind would fill
and my mouth would sing
what fills my mind,
and any human face
that crosses my face
would be happy
knowing my mind
was moving again,
knowing I was I again.
But I am not I again.
I am less I than I ever was.

*

And what if it's not I
in the snow?
if it's my son there?
if I am not I
but a human face crossing,
watching his mind let go?
if the snow were not snow
but a storm in his mind,
a flame set loose by exposure?
if he were sunk in his mind
and the storm of his mind
and not the snow?
if everyone stepped back
and watched him go?

WINTER STREET

No day when some part of you,
a part
previously unknown

feverdust absentia	splendor floe	bacterial regalia
feverdust absentia	splendor floe	bacterial regalia
feverdust absentia	splendor floe	bacterial regalia

See how things break down?

The body is a money pit
for the soul.

*

The river cuts
the fingers
of any hand
that presses.
A monochrome
sever
for the moon's
sorry finale.
No rock, no stone,
just a broken
stutter of
of.

*

A corpse can dance, of course,
if you hold it up, bear
its dwindling weight
across the kitchen floor.
What other partner
would become lighter
as the music pours?
A petal-shedding flower?
A leaky jug of water?
An open bag of sugar?
Nothing can force
skin to the interior.
It will shred before.
It's the exterior
that last flowers.
It's everything else
that follows.

*

A dog stands on its porch
barking at the door,
the heat churns on,
a door closes.
                        Is closed.
May the plane
shaking the air
pass quickly by—

orphan sky with so much
slipping through its fingers.

*

The broken plow
with its broken blade
stuck on the side
of the broken street—

vaccine delivery system

one street pocked
for the good of the other streets

*

The sun-slicked path
borrows its direction
from the river, pocked
with ice-crops and snow.
Ice-corpse and snow.
One stone has been cut
clean through the center,
the inner meat removed,
now notch through which.
Further downstream, a stone
is sandwiched between chunks
of ice. The water moves
coldly around it.

*

The frozen river moves
forward and out, up
and out—
the water beneath the ice
takes its usual course,
the ice swells toward
minimum resistance,
toward sky, then bank.
Neither will converge
though both collapse
into the river
as the river rises
and spreads. Winter
flood or winter street,
every surface
slick and, for us,
for now, impassable.

*

The silver bridge
with its silver span—
in every cut of light
it's silver, spun
across the water
at the curve.
The curve is not silver,
nor is the water.
Winter, here,
is silver, holds silver
in its silver bridge.

MOTH ARK

Mere minion of light,
lit, as in liturgy, as in
light, luster a lesser
source of light, a lack.
Locked onto light, moth
minion looks to matter,
the making of matter
by light its lot, light's
lot. Lacking light, moth
looks, lacks less when
it collides: moth and light,
ark of light, moth ark.

*

Light the binder, myth
now emotion. Mass moves
with light, mood moves,
is moved by light. What light
binds, mood lights. What
myth lights, doom binds.
Light binds mood to myth,
doom moves mood to light.

*

Color recedes, the eye
combines. Color combines
to recede. To cover color
with mood. Cover with mood.
Mood recedes to myth.

*

The senses removed,
unmoored and turned
to face those facing them.
The senses picked over,
perceived as senses, sans
organs, sans human thing.
The human thing
unbodied and thinged,
the senses received
without and not within
the shell. The human
plastic shell.

*

The plastic has weight
and is real. The plastic
has substance. The substance
has texture. The plastic exists
through texture. Forms arise
and recede, advance with color
and recede. Tactile plastic
pleasure, the eye traces,
moves with what moves.
Plastic motion, plastic journey.

*

Objects gray as they recede,
blend with the air and haze.
Cold recedes, the warm haze
advances. To push back
the colder, colorless air.

*

Beauty distorts, is
a distortion. Terror,
too, distorts.
The plastic message.

CARNAL MARSH

Up against
a shorn mass
once called
my body,
my body
collides with,
becomes one with
that which rolls.

TAKEN, TAKEN

When what remains is dirty
remnants—dirty snow, dirty slush
(yes, even the ice is dirty)—
we stroll the world's paltry
offerings as if to look
for a ribbon of color buried
somewhere in the shared
object of our hatred.
We, resigned to find
nothing not sullied,
are not disappointed.

WINTER SONGS

The piss on the tree
is no statement.
The piss on the snow.
Beneath, leaves
slobber the earth.

*

Neither
destroyed
nor created,
only moved.
From there
to there.
Less here,
more there.

*

I pull at my face,
at the branch in my face.
Am served a sodden song.
Swerve a ridden wrong.
There are no eyes for this.

*

There is so much more sky
now. So much more gray
in the sky now. More
pain in the sky now.

*

To shiver past your prime
an ice-dappled chore.
Forget what happened
the winter before.
Forget and forebear,
the path runs right through you.
The packed, immaculate path.

*

Bent sky over a bent house,
erase what will not announce
itself under the sun's clear eye.
Drag it all down to melt.
Piles and piles of melt.

*

My clumpstrangled hair,
my icicled cock and guitar-
curled nose drip upon entrance.
Drip after the application
of compressed violence.
Of course there's nothing left.
A seeping loss, burned, bereft.

*

Hit the ground running.
Hit the ground.
Hit the face in front of you.
Hit the tree and its window, too.
A broken toy, no please
or thank you.
Welcome to this ditch
with a view.

*

Honk at the swarm
at the feeder, aim
for the swarm.
Don't ever say it's cold.
Don't call this a problem.
Let's cross the icy bridge
arm in arm in arm.

*

Snow is never silent,
it pokes as it falls.
This common house
can feel every flake.
Once the snow stops
it's silent.
But then it's not snow,
it's not snowing.
As when the rain stops,
it's not raining.
The sun etcetera.
The fog, the clouds,
the bliss etcetera.

*

What the roof holds
is not weight but
the illusion of weight
corralled
and condensed.
The gutters peak,
the shingles speak,
the shutters creak.
I wait all day
for something to break.

*

What night brings
is not brought at all.

*

The snow makes the same mistake
twice. Strikes the same place
twice. You have it so wrong:
we go into the ditch by choice.
Our dream there is to ride.

*

Where *sick* means *wicked*
means something like *good*
cubed, where flatness is
not only desired but needed,
where a solitary shudder
can be kept to oneself,
ditto error, ditto fall,
where *garish* means *tacky*
means Christmas all
around me, 12025
Mountain Mountain Drive,
the number's unlisted
but fuck it: unfound me.

WINTER BLIND

the sun reflecting
sends a shiver

pierces the eye
even in shade

ELEGY ELEGY

The dead keep coming back to us
whether we will their return or not:

in our sleep, when we slip to resist,
in books, and in song, when the voice

shuffles forward to call "I'm still alive /
I win the prize / I'm still alive,"

even though he's not, even though
he knew that his song some day would prove

false, a sometime untrue statement
that no one, not even a ghost,

can retract. Instead, those of us left
are left to notice, and miss, and hurt.

How thin is the human voice,
it cannot keep even the dead

distant, on the other side of any
thing we would call any thing.

BRITTLE TRAVEL

The iced-
over
river
fingers
the water
slowly
grunting
beneath it.
A bird's eye
below, stuck
until spring
cranks this
view
back
into flow.
Welcome
to the present
private
disaster.
Every thing
a scatter-
shot
bargain.
Your spot
is secure.

*

To be
trapped
under ice
as in a river
as in a pond
fit for skating
only inches
between water
and air
between there
and there
there is no way
to eat
your way through

to be drowning
and feel thirsty

                             thirstier

*

What kind
of fall
finds you here

a crash through the ice
a slip at the bank
a blind or drunken step

or was there no fall
and you simply awoke
in some ceilinged pool
the hand in front
of your face
an arm poised
to hold you out
or bail you under

*

What organ encased
in the floating ice,
surface deceit
held fast
and punctured—
no breath can hold
its weight in here
down here,
the ice darker
than the depths
despite the sun's
yawning caress
of the exposed
and moving field

*

A note
from a piano
first key
then chord
then held—
an assault
on silence,
ice's silence
and dwell,
a ringing
performed
from below
and above,
a ringing
withheld
in water
and ear,
in ear
and ice—

*

Ice moss

Ice vine

The green
offers
an exit
a trail the eye
can trace
and the rest
can follow
a pulsing   pushing
you pushing
against the ice

                             into the green

the bird's eye
your eye

*

The route out

                                        squeeze your view
                                        into a squint
                                        that will fit
                                        into the eye
                                        stuck before you
                                        squeeze your self
                                        into the silver
                                        bird eye blinding
                                        the ice as
                                        it gives in
                                        to the pressure
                                        of eye's green

will undo you

*

As ice cannot contain
or absorb
you skitter through
—pocket of air to pocket of air—
until the ice is below you
along with the body
you no longer want
or need
and deaf to your self
and its sounds
you let the wind work
on you, deliver you
to wherever wind
wants (you) to go

*

You
a mite
in the eye
that killd the bird
a mote
to be fingerd
out and tossd aside
a note
concussd
until the ear
snuffs out
and sound turns
fog
harassing the ice

WINTER PASTURE

Here he comes with his day breath
and maximum air

some awkward two-step
no fowl would abide

What bitter apple
spread across his lips

What alabaster   What shine

The path to his door
a trammeled expanse

Deliver him now
to what he most wants

An arc between two points
on this flat absent surface

Deliver him now

A shape coming into view
the light rips right through it

Everything shifts
when the glare shreds it

*

Here he comes with his day face
a swollen construct of bee-stung skin

Guide him by hoof   by hand
to what he most needs

static shimmer
in the periphery

static shimmer
in front

Who'll call for clouds
to shield the eye

Not him   you say
There is no way

Some kind of metamorphosis
at work here

To call a horse a he

The land is always flat
the grass brown and low

An open expanse
filled with nothing

*

Here he comes with his vivisection frown
a bundle of nerves ripe for dismantle

Hang him on that hook
he will drain toward the edges

de ojos de caballo que tiemblan en la noche

Dead when you hang him
dead when you drain him

The body a tesseract
by virtue of angle

The floor here is tilted
please step away from the blood

*

Here he comes with his clipboard
and case notes

dentures intact   jaw outturned

How to read what cannot be worded
a spell that spins the human out

A sound from the throat
unburrowed

The wind when it comes
will carry it

hang it on that hook
drift toward the edges

WINTER STATIC

They dig and seek what they cannot corner

                              or gather

a barricade of gloves carried abottom

this staircase slipped with ice

first leaves now snow

                              scraped off and thrown

to the side to exchange scrunch for slick

*

They pivot and catch what they're compelled to release

no further down without a point

                                        to press

displace

                move air to ice

air to grind and erase   disappear

what for now occupies air's space

*

They flock and bother what they cannot flee

the water stuck in its throne   listing

as if solid it must be   float or floe

on the river river road   moving

road   moving river

                                        road

*

They rock and shutter what they feel they must cease

some sliver of water dangling fine

no drip

some sliver to impress on the ground its need

to rise above itself itself and carry what has no desire

to go

*

They fathom and totter what they face down in toto

                                        or intact

a minor movement and series

                              a flagrancy of fact

no sooner or later than nothing or now

the sound a drift   a sullied bespect

the lens a fracture of light and despond

*

They shriek and shimmy what they feel obliged to borrow

as a friend will remove and never return

the lack a ring that grows over time

a word skirts   stalls the matter

a final celestial sidewalk strummed choir

*

I borrow your brother and blink all atangent

my stickerish limbs know the price of a fall

no parting or such fielding these questions

the ice when it melts will right what is sinking

a torn apart bargain for any still standing

*

I wring and deform that which is lodged

the hand a cradle for anything swollen

oh please don't befriend or relieve me

this freeze-shattered fact a matter of ache

buried until plain speech won't arouse it

*

I shake and I shake   the liquid now streaming

a full-headed fright the road is all closed

no lanterns or godsends to burrow me forward

sheets and drifts guide the discarded

a foreseen insensate puddled beneath me

*

The wheels of the burden a curtain of precip

no sight emerges to cull the collected

the snow   do you see it   it covers

itself a snow-covered font

the blend is what   in the end   fills us

*

This they I posit   this you   some we

what I to deliver or beg for inspect

when all I require is an hour for slumber

a pillow of wet   a blanket of ice

a surface still and unchanging

*

Come   someone says   loudly   with gust

we huddle   this I   a snow-stricken force

come   someone says   and we collect as if pulled

a shore-twisted alabast minus the rust

some gargle of bodies

                         this topple of us

*

Come   someone says   they will be here

                                           in breath

a backward entice to shriek us all forward

come   someone says   we the sore-appled

a dimness is arcing its falling in our direction

a stillness of ice   a performance unfrozen

*

The view we are left with   a silicon vision

the words and their colors all undressed in the cold

everything soon will be numbered   yawned open

unless the illusion of movement reclaims its divide

decreases our sorrows   you static

                                        you snow

NOTES

"River Border": "Rivers grind borders into dust" (Erik Anderson, *The Poetics of Trespass*).

The title of and italicized passages in "Bright Inviting" are from Medbh McGuckian.

"Moth Ark" is built on phrases from Mark Rothko's *The Artist's Reality: Philosophies of Art*.

The title of "Carnal Marsh" is from M.P. Shiel's *The Purple Cloud*.

The title of "Taken, Taken" is from James Schuyler.

"Elegy Elegy" is for Vic Chesnutt.

The italicized phrase in "Winter Pasture" is from Octavio Paz's "Agua nocturna."